MW00723494

HEART CHECK

A Poetry Book

Tiese M. Bridges

Foreword by Dorothy Welch

First Edition 2020
Printed in the United States of America
First Printing 2020
First Edition 2020
ISBN- 978-0-578-59573-3
10 9 8 7 6 5 4 3 2 1

Book cover designed by Tiese Bridges of Tbridge Graphics
Email: Tbridgegraphics@gmail.com
Instagram and Facebook: @Tbridgegraphics
Author Instagram: @Tiesebridges
Website: Tiesebridges.com
Photo of Author by James R. McPhatter Jr.
of James McPhatter Photography
Instagram: @Jamesmcphatterphotography
Website: Macvphoto.com

Edited by Tiese M. Bridges, Calvis McLaurin, & Deana Johnson

Dedication

To Denise Darnelle Dunn, the woman who taught me what I know about writing, who planted the seeds way back in my days working alongside her at the library. She was, unbeknownst to her and myself, helping to birth my first book. I will forever cherish what I learned from her teachings.

God rest her beautiful, creative, childlike soul.

Contents

"The pen is mightier than the sword"

-Edward Bulwer-Lytton

Foreword

My, my, my! First, I would like to express my deepest gratitude for this young, gifted Woman of God and for allowing me to contribute to the first of many projects, is an honor. *Heart Check* is truly an amazing manuscript. Tiese has taken tender parts of her life and opened them up that others may experience the unfathomable love and forgiveness of the Almighty God. Whatever age we may be, this book will definitely witness to a time in our lives that we just didn't think we would recover, especially from a broken heart. Her style of writing is unique and relatable in every word that shows up on the pages. I invite you to take this journey from beginning to end with *Heart Check*; and when you emerge from this book, I promise you will experience more faith, solid freedom, and a fresh love for yourself and God that will never be shaken again! ♥

Dorothy Welch "Pastor D."
Gentle Breeze Ministries

As I reviewed the poetry written, I'm reminded of David and his ability to express his feelings with such vulnerability to God. As David did in the book of Psalm, I have expressed myself and opened doors that I only wanted God to enter...until now. I have bared my soul naked in hopes that it will provoke healing and encouragement to you, the reader. To the person reading this book, know that God is capable of doing far beyond what you may see and are experiencing at this season in your life. In the words of David,

"Wait on the Lord: be of good courage and he shall strengthen your heart, wait I say on Lord." (Psalm 27:14)

Pain

Pain makes you creative.

Pain births vision.

Pain is motivating.

Pain transforms you into a tool for help.

Pain speaks...listen to it.

Don't reject it. Embrace it. PIMP IT!

Untie this tie that was intertwined by the wrapping of our thighs.

Untie this bondage; untie this stronghold.

Untie thoughts of the memories we made. My mind is all knotted up.

I realize I can't ask God to untie this soul tie if I refuse to give Him the rope.

A puppeteer's string I feel I'm connected to at times.

I'm being controlled by these sexual desires.

I know it's been nearly a year now and if it were to present itself again...mmm, I'm not sure I would decline.

I deny my sanity, I deny my healing, and I deny my growth, if I allow his hands to grope what's supposed to be a living sacrifice.

A sacrifice I made when I laid and a covenant wasn't made.

A sacrifice that cost more than I was willing to pay.

No ring, but definitely a ring of repeated cycles.

I became no longer a slave to the Savior, but a slave to premarital sex.

Help me God to exit this out of my life before I spiritually lose it!

It's fogging my view of you, and it's getting thicker.

Untie this soul connected. Untie me.

Clear my vision so I can see your true meaning of what sex is meant to be.

May I never part my legs again in harmony, until I've walked down the aisle in Holy matrimony.

Untouchable

I can't touch you. I'm literally 8 feet away from your room, and I can't touch you. I hear your voice, and I still can't hear you. I see your face, and I still can't see you. Can you see me? Am I visible to you at all?

Does my true heart's posture show through the mask I use to hide what it really is? We're in each other's presence, hiding the truth in the depths of our hearts. If we're to act on these feelings, it would end in sin and that I don't want.

If the truth came to, our hearts posture would say "I want you."

But the heart is deceitful above all things right? (Jeremiah 17:9).

So I'll end this here, and I'll be here if it's meant to be, but if it's not I'll openly accept the destiny that God has for me and this poem will only become a memory of what I once wished could be-

You and I.

It's the next day, and she still smells the scent of his saliva on her top lip from when she kissed him goodbye. A night of conversation led to fornication. Knowing she knew better, knowing there had been others before her with no guard, no regards to her commitment to God, never mind that! No regards to the other women she witnessed from a far...FOOLS! That fell for his looks and charm. I guess she was an even bigger one. She was leading the pack. Round and around and around they went that night, the pleasure she felt surpassed the conviction in her spirit. She just wanted to release all of the pain, all of the hurt., even if that meant being held by the one who was full of deceit. The very shoulder she laid on turned on her, but she still wanted him, her heart still desired those texts from him saying "May I see you." Saying yes to those messages meant consent..."Yes, you may hurt me again," "Yes, you can break my heart even more. Here's the hammer." 2 years later and enough was enough; this time was going to be different. As she laid, fetal position, on her living room floor, Bible clutched to her chest, disheveled hair, mopping the floor with her tears as her red robe moved across every drop. When will the pain end? How does she get out of this? She's tired. She wants to believe there is light at the end, but this black hole she created was so deep that she couldn't see. With fasting, came strength and boldness. She finally confessed. She fled from the place that caused much trauma and anxiety and was destined for a place that helped set her free and healed her heart entirely. Going back to the battlefield where she was wounded, no longer smelled of the blood from her former broken heart, but of victory, peace, and joy because she survived. She survived rejection, she survived the lies, she survived deceit, she survived being crushed and because of it, the oil is flowing heavily now.

To the men and women who've been "church hurt", don't run away from the church because I guarantee it is an element the Lord will use to help heal you. Maybe your pain was self-inflicted like mine due to disobedience or maybe you did nothing to cause the pain that you're experiencing. I want you to know-It. Will. End. "When?" you ask...I don't know. What I do know is you must stay the course, you must endure. Don't let your pain be in vain. Use it for the advancement of others and yourself. Someone is waiting on you to get through, so that you can get them through. Just as I did, one day you will say..."It was good that I was afflicted" (Psalm 119:71).

Before Destruction

A shell of shame he was enclosed in because of the pain he caused another, the guilt was too heavy to cope with, so he hid.

He didn't realize he was already forgiven; he didn't realize he was no longer a prisoner of his past decisions.

He didn't realize the true freedom Christ was ready to release, if he gave up the pride, that he guarded inside. A crisis he was in because he never dealt with his sin.

A cycle he went in because he was never willing to admit his faults and repent.

They say pride comes before the fall.

I pray God's mercy softens the ground he lands on.

Tittle Tattle

Mouths open, words come out. When they are loosely spoken, you never know what they'll hit. An emotional trigger they can be, when not used wisely. Do they know what they're saying? Do they know the damage they've done? Their mouths are chambers and their words are bullets, shooting and creating holes in the souls of others. Even fools are considered wise when they keep silent...so what does that make them? Hold your fire; put your mouth on safety. Let your words be as delicate as rose petals and not as painful as the stem of thorns they grow on. Speak with ease, speak with care. Don't let your words be as a roaring lion with intent to kill its prey, but let your speech be like Jesus-edifying, healing, and loving.

"Obedience is better than sacrifice."

The word says this for a reason.

You never know what it is you're sacrificing; your joy, your spiritual strength, your peace of mind, or even your very life.

The Holy Spirit warns us when something isn't right, so why is that we go left? Ask yaself.

I'll Be Damned

Romans 13:2- "Whosoever therefore resisteth the power, resisteth the ordinance of God: and they that resist shall receive to themselves **damnation**".

So what do I do? Go back to what I'm used to.

In weakness sex, in pain pacify it with a man I'm not even truly interested in. Go back to sexing my ex that's no longer mine, but a man that belonged to someone else. I'll be damned if I do that. So what do I do? Do I have a pity party? Cry out to God why and how much I don't believe this is going to work out for my good. It's all good. No its not. It's all bad, I cried, but yet I didn't cling to you. I used the things of this world to suppress the true intent of my heart. I was broken, and I was tired of pretending.

Tired of trying to numb the pain, by not dealing with it. So what did I do?

I surrendered. I surrendered my heart, body and soul. No premarital sex, no connection with anything that was detrimental to my spirit man.

I engulfed myself day by day in the word of God. My heart was sick, dying and starving for you. And my flesh is telling me to go backwards?? NO, I climbed to you. My strength, my healer, my peace, my desire, my joy, Abba father, El Shada, Jehovah Nissi, Elohim, to name a few, that translates all to the matchless character of God, yes You.

It was in You, that I gained my victory and I will forever keep You near.

I dare not go back to the person I used to be.

I'll be damned if I do that.

9

When we meet. heaven will smile. God will smile because his vision is nearly complete.

Two souls on the same mission.

Two lives joining together as one.

When we meet it'll be a friendship, a connection so deep that even we can't comprehend it.

We'll let the leading of the Holy Spirit take us where we may go and we won't take a step without Him. When we meet and surpass the stage of friendship into our covenant with God and each other, we will change the world.

Looking to God to give us our strength and direction.

Portraying His love to all through our love for each other.

Love will take on a new definition for me, for us. It will be one love, one heartbeat, one goal, one savior that rescued us from the old that was falsely masked as true love but was ultimately a false sense of it.

On that day, two rings shall become one infinite circle. God shall be pleased.

His ordained plan for His two children will have come to pass, to fulfill an even greater purpose.

We will know true love, a 1 Corinthians 13 kind of love.

A God love, when we meet.

Sorry if I'm being a bit skeptical during our courtship stage. I'm scared due to the past and not quite sure on how to handle long response times and your silent moments on the phone.

I wonder what you're thinking. Is it me?

I'm sorry these insecurities are spilling over into what's supposed to be you and I. What should be two, is now a crew of three.

My thoughts party in my head, jumping, screaming, and singing lies.

It's hard for me to fight them at times and I end up joining them...

To make matters worse I become the life of the party.

You see I'm scared to admit this to you, out of fear that I'll push you away.

A part of me wants you to know and the other doesn't.

How do I tell you I still have parts of me that are broken? How do I say I need reassurance that you're here for me? The authentic me.

How do I tell you I question your every move because you seem too good, to be true? I'm ashamed to mention these things.

Vulnerability and I don't have that great of a relationship at times.

Polar opposites we are, but what empty spaces the puzzles of our lives are missing, we have it for each other, joining together creating a majestic portrait.

You amaze me. You cover me in prayer and tell me the truth in love.

I gain an abundance of wisdom from the wisdom God has graced you with.

My spirit has been electrified because of our connection.

Show me you got me, Show me consistency. Show me you'll cover my heart. Show me I'm safe with you. No worries...Ill do the same too.

It's been said "opposites attract" so let's see what this does. There's a war in my mind and it's intensifying in its brutality. The weakness within stands no chance against the villainous presence of this enemy. Blackouts occur with intent to demolish all notions of positivity and in the corner of my mind there I sit feeling screwed and my negative thoughts were the drill. I'm not even sure if going on the fast will help this ordeal. I'm too weak! Issues I tell myself I have every time I let you win, over and over again with every comparison with every compliment I didn't get. One up for you, zero for me. One stab to the heart, one shot to the head and in an instant I'm losing and my strength is fading. Like an instant Polaroid pic, someone come and shake me out of this despair. Never have I felt so low like a serpent crawling the ground seeking whom he can devour, these thoughts devour me causing all hell in my mind, borderline crossing the suicide line, you refuse to let me cross, reminding me that that's exactly what He died on. He reminded me of what He did over 2000 years ago, saying "I die for this, I died for you". He shed His blood, to cover my blood so that my mind could be completely free from this monster I invited in called insecurities. He secured me with every hammering of a nail into His feet, with every bang of a nail to His hand, piercings to His side, multiple whips on His back... "Thy will be done" He prayed so that we could be saved. You see his love for me runs so deep that even I can love me. His love for us so deep, that we can love ourselves.

13

They say opposites attract and indeed they do. In the book of Matthew, Jesus willingly attracted His body to the cross to die for me. For you.

Thank you Jesus for dying for our insecurities.

Love is patient, love is kind, love is never boastful or full of pride.

Love is Christ stretching His arms wide to die for you.

Multiple whips on his back for you...that's love.

Hammering into His feet for you...that's love.

Bangs into His hands for you...that's love.

Love is Art.

His body representing the brush.

His blood representing the paint.

The cross representing the canvas, all intended for our sins to be forgiven.

I love you, saith the Lord and nothing can void this.

Recognize you have a king in your midst.

Who created the sun? I. Who created the Stars? I. Who created the very soil you walk on? I. Who created you? I. I love you, can't you see?

All I want is your everything; is that too much for me?

Is it too much to say good morning to me first, instead of your phone?

Is it too much to ask for more of your time?

I get nostalgic at times; I recollect the memories I had with you in the beginning of your salvation, when you desired the sincere milk of my word.

I was number one on your list.

What happened to our fellowship? I miss you!

What happened to the times that the altar was the first place you hit on a Sunday morning?

Though you left me, I never left you.

Don't you dare let the enemy tell you any different.

I love you and nothing can separate you from that, my word is true.

I hear your heart. I know you! In times when you felt the lowest because of the weight from the sin, it was then that I kept you. It was then that my grace and mercy prevailed all the more.

I stretched my arms even greater to receive you back in.

What's love you ask?

This is love. I am love. I AM GOD.

I stand before you a once insecure, broken hearted woman, lost and bound to sin. Years ago, I was invited to a place that forever changed my life. Refuge was that place. A place that prized the very two people that would have a vital part to do with my destiny. That red kiss imprint on my checks and the deliverance in a woman's hug...That sincere "How's it going my friend" from a giving, and caring man of God is what kept me returning Sunday after Sunday.

A man and a woman who trusted the gift inside of me to deem me worthy as the marketing director, minister, and usher of the vision called Refuge of Deliverance. Deliverance is truly what I experienced.

Once insecure, now confident. Once weak, now strong. Once broken, now healed. A place where I discovered my strength, my worth, and my buried gifts. I thank you Apostle Daniel and Pastor Devetta White. Seven years of attending your ministry and I've elevated beyond what I imagined and it's because of the love of God in you. Because of you two, I am an oak tree...unmovable and rooted. I am warrior; I am a BEAST!

I back down from the enemy no more, and finally I am a true woman of God. When my season has come to an end and you're no longer my leaders, you will still be my leaders because of what you all have permeated in my soul. No you didn't do everything correct, but how can I expect you to? You still live in the flesh, just as I, but that's when grace and mercy steps in and covers. I pray you all will continue to be spiritually aware, forever growing in the knowledge of

God and ministry. May you never let promotion snatch your humbleness, and may you forever keep those smiles.

I love you both.

The day, the minute, the second, the moment, I decided to leave, you came after me.

The moment I decided to choose sin over you, you came after me.

The moment I rejected you, you still accepted me. I didn't have to earn it. You gave it freely. Oh, how you love me, but oh, what a mess I am and still you decide in all of your majesty and all of your grace and all of your mercy, take the scattered puzzle pieces of my heart and put it back together.

I've come to realize that after all of the fulfilling I attempted to do for my soul, that you God are the only one that's needed.

You're the only glass that I can continuously drink from even when it looks empty.

You are the only one that allows me to walk on water, even when the waves of life seem as high as the heavens.

You are the only one that saw the blood of guilt on my hands, cleansed them with your mercy and said "my son's forgiving blood covers that."

My heart is marked with the saving cross in the center, dripping with your redemption.

You have filled the void.

Sin can no longer employ here.

I hear your word. I meditate on it and it's locked in.

I discarded the key and I'm never letting it flee.

Unquestionably free I am and free I will forever be.

My heart is che✔ked. No exit from me when my God comes knocking.

He's here. Knock, knock. "Let me in".

I did. My heart has been checked. I win!

To my "Heart Checkers"...Come to the end of "self" and let him do it for you too.

Acknowledgment: A poem

I acknowledge the loss. I acknowledge the hurt. You may feel like your life is being buried, like a body in a hearse, but I promise, stay the course and that pain will be reversed.

I see the bruises. I see the scars. I see the tear drops falling from your eyes, creating a sea that you feel like you're drowning in. Let me share this with you, It ends. You will win. You will be whole again. Smile again. Feel again. No longer numb. No longer bound from the internal weights within. That's it, press in. Breathe again.

Live again. Inhale, exhale. You feel that? Life is now new for you again.

I see your heart. I see your pain.

I acknowledge you, and the wisdom you will gain after this.

I acknowledge that this couldn't have been possible without God the Lover of my soul the one who says I am the apple of His eye, the one who I am most precious to. I thank Him for the gifts that He has given me to share with the world. This is for His glory alone and His glory alone.

To my leaders Apostle Daniel and Pastor Devetta White:
Apostle, thank you for giving me the motivation to start and finish this book. Because of the production of your three books, a fire ignited in me that wouldn't die down until this book was complete. I love you both. Continue smiling through and being the "oak trees" you all are.

To my parents, Michael Bridges and Sylvia Williams. If it weren't for you two, I wouldn't be here and Heart Check would not have been birthed. Thanks for having relations over 29 years ago. ☺

To God's secret weapon in my life, Pastor D!!! You are my angel in the flesh. Thank you for being my "butterfly"...bold, free, colorful, and gentle.

To Cuh (Roteshia), Latonya, Shakiea, Jasper, Tawanda, and my new found sister in Christ Talyah. God used the anointing in you all to help destroy the yokes of bondage off my life. I'm so blessed to have you.